WHEN SUFFER

MW01045585

Finding Purpose in Pain

Ron Rhodes

Harold Shaw Publishers
Wheaton, Illinois

ISBN 0-87788-929-5

Cover © Luci Shaw

98 97 96 95 94 93 92

10 9 8 7 6 5 4 3

Contents

Introduction

After an extensive tour across the United States, the famous German pastor and theologian Helmut Thielicke was asked what he saw as the greatest defect among American Christians. He replied quite simply, "They have an inadequate view of suffering."

Could Thielicke be correct? Perhaps. How often pastors hear questions like: "Do you think my cancer is an indication that God is mad at me and is getting even?" "Why did God cause our little girl to be hit by a car and die? Has he done this to strengthen our faith?" or, "How can you say that God is all-powerful and all-loving when he doesn't bother to prevent innocent babies from dying of AIDS?" Such questions remind me of the bitter comment by H. G. Wells that God is "an ever-absent help in time of trouble."

Blaise Pascal once said that it is the fate of God to be everlastingly misunderstood. Questions such as those above are an indication that people have misunderstood God and that an adequate philosophy for dealing with pain and suffering is sorely lacking.

Of course, not just any philosophy will do. Life's most complex problems rarely have simple answers. Only a philosophy based on the timeless truths contained in Scripture accomplishes the twofold goal of (1) ensuring that Christians will not misunderstand the nature of God and (2) enabling Christians to make sense of human pain and suffering. Any philosophy that accomplishes less is inadequate.

Do you sometimes feel as though God doesn't care about you and is ignoring your pain? Do you ever conclude that your faith must be deficient because no miracle has come? Do you sometimes suspect that God may be sending painful experiences because you are such a bad sinner? Do you ever secretly doubt that God is truly all-powerful and all-loving? If so, you aren't alone.

This studyguide can serve as a road map for cutting through some of the confusion and misunderstanding surrounding human pain and suffering. No doubt there are some questions which will remain unanswered until you enter into glory, but meanwhile God has not left you to grope around blindly in a world of pain. He has given you all you *need* to know in his Word. Understanding what he has to say about this issue is your birthright as a believer. May God give you his joy and comfort as you claim this birthright.

How to Use this Studyguide

The purpose of this studyguide is to provide penetrating questions that will enable you to understand what Scripture has to say about the purpose of suffering. Some of these questions will direct your attention to what the text *says*. Others will ask you to focus on the *meaning* of the text. Still others will ask you to *apply* what you learn to your life. These questions recognize that people remember most what they discover for themselves and what they express in their own words.

Each study is planned for an hour-long discussion. If your group opts for a time of prayer, sharing, and/or socializing, add on an appropriate amount of time for these activities. Try to stick to time limits, and keep distractions to a minimum.

Group members should recognize that the leader is a *question-asker* and not an *answer-person*. The answers are in the Bible passage. Accordingly, different members should feel free to take part in leading the discussion.

Volunteer leaders should be familiar with the Scripture text and the direction of the questions in order to guide the discussion and keep the study on target. Leaders should be careful not to talk too much. The "traffic pattern" of the group should not be leader/group member/leader/group member (like a question-answer time), but should flow naturally and freely among group members. Leaders who keep too tight a rein on the discussion tend to make group interaction rigid and mechanical. Remember that maximum participation means maximum learning.

SUGGESTIONS FOR GROUP MEMBERS

1. Each person should own a copy of the studyguide.

2. Before beginning, ask the Lord for wisdom. He promises to give it if you ask (James 1:5). Ask the Lord to show you applicable truths for your daily life. Your goal for this study is a changed life.

3. In preparation for the discussion, read the passage(s) several times, preferably in different translations, such as the *New International Version*, the *New American Standard Bible*, the *Revised Standard Version*, and *The New English Bible*. After reading the assigned verses, answer the questions in the guide.

4. Approach each study intending to discover new insights. Don't just formulate smooth answers you can present to the group.

5. Stick to the passage under discussion. Don't jump around, looking up every verse that comes to mind. Let the assigned passage *speak for itself.* If the passage needs additional background, the guide will point you to relevant verses.

6. Try to avoid tangents. If you sense the discussion drifting off target, feel free to ask, "Are we on the subject?" Or, "Could we finish the discussion and talk about this issue later?"

7. Keep the Bible as the authority in the group—not the leader, the studyguide, or a Bible commentary.

8. Listen to other group members. If you are shy or slow to speak, keep in mind that the group needs to hear your insights. You may see something in the text that no one else sees. If you are naturally talkative, deliberately discipline yourself to give shyer members a chance to contribute.

9. Resist side conversations.

10. Make specific, personal applications for your life, not general ones for the whole world. Don't be afraid to make yourself vulnerable by being honest about your needs with the group.

Your openness will encourage others to do likewise.

SUGGESTIONS FOR GROUP LEADERS

1. Prepare in advance. Read the passage; answer each question; plan your time.

2. Begin and end the study at the agreed time.

3. Begin your discussion session with a brief prayer. Avoid calling on someone by surprise. Not everyone feels comfortable praying in public, so ask someone ahead of time if you can call on him or her.

4. Ask for a volunteer to read the passage aloud.

5. Read the first question and wait for an answer. Don't be afraid of silences; sometimes group members ponder a few moments before answering. Resist the temptation to answer the question yourself, or group members will think they don't have to participate. If necessary, restate or rephrase the question.

6. Some studies include helpful quotations or explanatory notes. These should be read *after* the group discussion on the preceding question is completed.

7. If a question in the guide has already been answered in the course of the discussion, skip it and move on.

8. Keep the Bible as the authority, not yourself. If someone asks you a question, put it to the group, or point to relevant Scripture passages that address the issue.

9. The best discussion leader is not a *teacher* but a *moderator*. Your job is not to lecture, but to encourage discussion.

10. Encourage group participation. Ask questions like, "Are there other ideas?" Or, "What does someone else think?"

11. If the discussion moves off the subject, draw the group back to the passage by restating the question, or by asking what a particular verse says about the subject. The only allowable "off-the-subject" topic is, "What is a real Christian and how do you become one?"

12. Receive all answers warmly. If someone's answer is off base, ask, "In which verses did you find that?" Or, "What does someone else think?"

13. Encourage shy members to speak. Look for hints in facial expressions. You might ask, "Can we hear from someone who hasn't spoken up yet?"

14. If someone in the group is talking too much, ask group members to think quietly about a question. Then ask, "Can someone who hasn't spoken yet give us an idea?"

15. For more information on the dynamics of group study and inductive study, consult Gladys Hunt's *You Can Start a Bible Study Group*, available from Harold Shaw Publishers, Box 567, Wheaton, Illinois, 60189.

STUDY ONE

Paradise Lost

Genesis 2:4–9, 15–25; 3

The name *Eden* is synonymous with *paradise*. Scholars associate it with a Hebrew word meaning "bliss" or "delight." God intended Eden to be a glorious, utopian garden for people to enjoy. But the unthinkable happened. The creature sinned against the Creator! And the Fall of Adam and Eve marked the entrance of pain and suffering into their little heaven on earth.

Ever since this catastrophic event, men and women the world over have grappled with perplexing questions like, "Where did evil come from?" and "How can there be a good God when terrible evil exists in the world?" The Book of Genesis (which means "beginnings") is the place to start in exploring answers to these and other questions.

1. How does it make you feel when you see innocent people suffer?

2. Read Genesis 2:4–9. Though God created people with the capacity to experience pain, what provisions did he make for a pleasurable, pain-free existence?

What does this tell you about the goodness of God and his will regarding humankind's happiness and fulfillment?

3. Read Genesis 2:15–17. The Hebrew word for "work" in verse 15 means "to serve." How might a person's fulfillment and happiness in life be related to work or service for the Creator?

4. With freedom comes responsibility (verses 16–17). Why does God's gift of freedom necessitate that he allow his creatures to experience the full consequences of their choices?

5. Read Genesis 2:18–25. God created people with a built-in need for intimate relationships. How does God make the perfect provision for insulating Adam from the pain of loneliness?

6. Read Genesis 3:1–7. What was Satan's strategy for luring Adam and Eve away from God? How does he still use this strategy on believers today?

7. Read Genesis 3:8–13. What effect did Adam and Eve's sin have on their relationship with God? How is this a form of pain?

How is their response an example of what *not* to do when one sins against God?

8. How do verses 8–13 show that God takes the initiative in seeking out people, even when they sin?

9. Read Genesis 3:14–19. We noted earlier that there are consequences (sometimes very painful ones) for the choices we make. How is this illustrated with the *serpent* (verses 14–15)? With *Eve* (verse 16)? With *Adam* (verses 17–19)?

10. Meditate a few moments on Genesis 3:15. What was God referring to when he told the serpent (Satan) that the woman's offspring "will crush your head, and you will strike his heel"?

11. Hebrews 2:14 describes Jesus in this way: ". . . so that by his death he might destroy him who holds the power of death—that is, the devil." In view of this, how does Genesis 3:15 show God's goodness and love for humankind in spite of the fact that Adam and Eve had just rebelled against him?

12. Read Genesis 3:20–24. How do the events described in these verses contribute to Adam and Eve's future prospects of suffering? How do they also represent God's mercy?

13. How has this study helped you to understand why pain and suffering exist in a world created by a good and loving God?

STUDY TWO

Legacy of the Human Race

Ecclesiastes 1–3:14; 4:1–8; 5:8–17

Paul W. Powell says that "trouble is not a gate-crasher in the arena of our lives; it has a reserved seat there" (*When the Hurt Won't Go Away*, 41). Every person is born into a world of pain and suffering because this is a *fallen* world. As a result of sin, humanity is alienated from God. This alienation guarantees that every person experiences at least *some* of what Solomon has described in Ecclesiastes. Suffering—in one form or another—is a corollary of fallen human existence. As Solomon learned by firsthand experience, this existence—lived apart from a relationship with the eternal living God—can lead only to despair.

1. Describe the time in your life when you first began to understand that life is not "a bed of roses."

Solomon is called "the Teacher" in Ecclesiastes 1:1. Solomon uses an extremely persuasive teaching method in Ecclesiastes. Throughout the book, he alternates between an *earthly perspective* (life "under the sun") and an *eternal perspective* that includes God. Solomon repeatedly demonstrates the despair that results from the *earthly perspective*. As the book progresses, the *eternal perspective* becomes the only viable option for survival in a fallen world wracked with pain.

2. Read Ecclesiastes 1. What did Solomon conclude about meaning in life for the person who seeks it apart from God (verses 1–11)? What type of pain does this person suffer?

---

3. Where did Solomon first seek refuge (verses 12–18)? How do people today do this?

---

4. Read Ecclesiastes 2:1–11. After the attainment of wisdom failed to meet Solomon's deepest needs, what course did he pursue? How do people today do this?

---

5. Read Ecclesiastes 2:17–26. What caused Solomon's despair? Why did he hate life?

In what way do these verses describe how life was for you before you came into a living relationship with Jesus Christ?

---

6. What do you see in these verses about the foolishness of putting all your efforts into transitory things?

---

7. Read Ecclesiastes 3:1–8. These verses suggest that both pain and joy are a routine part of human existence. Which of these "times" is a part of your experience right now? How does this passage help you understand these events?

---

8. Read Ecclesiastes 3:9–14. Verse 11 tells us that God has "set eternity in the hearts of men." How is the knowledge of our physical mortality and temporality a kind of pain? How does this pain motivate us to seek refuge in an eternal God?

---

9. Read Ecclesiastes 4:1–3. How much pain and suffering in the world is due to oppression of one kind or another? What are some specific contemporary examples of this?

10. Read Ecclesiastes 4:4–8. People are often discontent because of their desire to "keep up with the Joneses." How do these verses address this issue?

11. Read Ecclesiastes 5:8–17. In what ways can the love of money cause suffering in life?

12. In our brief look at Ecclesiastes, we have seen that suffering takes many forms. We noted earlier that Solomon alternates between an *earthly perspective* and an *eternal perspective* that includes God. He makes a strong case for the futility of the *earthly perspective*. Skip ahead to Ecclesiastes 12:13 and summarize Solomon's conclusion about living with an *eternal perspective* during this "short" time on earth.

13. What concrete steps can you begin taking this week to develop the eternal perspective?

STUDY THREE

A Reflection on God's Character?

Psalm 107:1–33

Bible scholar Norman L. Geisler asks, "Must one believe that God is cruel, compassionless, impotent, or nonexistent in order to deal with the reality of evil in the world?" He asserts that "this is more than an abstract, philosophical question. It touches each and every one of us where we live. And sooner or later, either deliberately or inadvertently, each of us adopts a view with regard to evil" (*Roots of Evil*, 12).

Many Christians have long struggled with the apparent paradox of how pain and suffering can exist in a world created by a benevolent and loving God.

C. S. Lewis commented that he would very much like to live in a universe governed by God in such a way that it could be said "a good time was had by all." "But since it is abundantly clear that I don't," said Lewis, "and since I have reason to believe, nevertheless, that God is Love, I conclude that my conception of love needs correction" (*Problem of Pain*, 40).

1. How would you respond to someone who asked you, "How can you believe in a benevolent and loving God when so much pain and suffering exists in the world?"

As a means of disciplining his rebellious children, God allowed Israel to go into exile in hostile Babylon. Then—after God accomplished his sovereign purpose—he delivered Israel from this Exile. Psalm 107 was written after Israel's return from the Babylonian Exile.

2. Read Psalm 107:1–3. How can the psalmist's statement that God's love "endures forever" be reconciled with the fact that he allowed Israel to suffer exile in Babylon?

3. Read Psalm 107:4–9. What do you see in verses 4–5 that suggests these individuals endured prolonged distress?

4. Because of their distress, these people cried out to God for deliverance (verse 6). According to verses 7–9, how did God *specifically* meet each of their needs as listed in verses 4 and 5?

What does this tell you about the *active nature* of God's enduring love?

5. Read Psalm 107:10–16. What brought on the suffering of this second group of individuals (verses 10–11)?

Is it legitimate for us to deduce from this that obedience to God's Word can prevent some painful events from occurring? Why or why not?

6. What conclusions can we draw about how God's discipline (verse 12) relates to his "unfailing love" (verse 15)?

7. Read Psalm 107:17–22. Do you think it is contradictory for a loving God to allow his children to experience the painful consequences of their wrong choices (verse 17)? Why or why not?

8. How do these verses illustrate that God may allow suffering because of its restorative value?

9. Read Psalm 107:23–33. Sometimes events that get out of control (from a human perspective) cause us to see our puniness. In what way do verses 25–30 indicate that the Lord sometimes designs events in our lives for the purpose of making us recognize our dependence on him? How is this compatible with his benevolence and love?

10. In view of what you have learned about the goodness of God, how might Psalm 107 strengthen your commitment to prayer (cf. verses 6, 13, 19, and 28)? To thanksgiving (cf. verses 1, 8, 15, 21, and 31)?

STUDY FOUR

Suffering for Righteousness

Acts 4:1–31; 6:8–15; 7:54–58; Matthew 5:10–12

When Jim Elliot was a college student in 1949, he wrote: "He is no fool who gives what he cannot keep to gain what he cannot lose" (Elisabeth Elliot, *Shadow of the Almighty*, 15). After college, Jim became a missionary in Ecuador to an unreached tribe of indians known as the Aucas. Because he loved them, he passionately desired to share with them the gospel of Jesus Christ. Yet it was at their hands that he and four other missionaries lost their lives. Jim and his friends knew what it meant to suffer for the gospel and for the sake of righteousness.

It is unlikely that most Christians will ever suffer for the sake of righteousness like Jim Elliot did. But to some extent, all Christians who genuinely seek to please God in their lives will sooner or later confront this type of suffering. In certain countries, persecution is an everyday occurrence for Christians. And it is distinctly possible that we may also face persecution in years to come.

1. How do you usually react when you are unfairly criticized or accused? Do you forgive and forget? Retreat in fear? Raise your defenses? Hold a grudge?

2. Read Acts 4:1–22. What precisely were Peter and John persecuted for?

3. Based on Peter and John's example, under what circumstances should Christians disobey human authorities (verses 18–20)?

What command of God represented a higher priority for Peter and John than the command issued by the Jewish authorities? (See Acts 1:8).

4. How do you reconcile Peter's words in verses 18–20 with his teaching on obedience to government in 1 Peter 2:13–17?

5. Read Acts 4:23–31. How did the believers respond to the threats by Jewish authorities?

As we examine the historical record of the early church in Acts, it becomes clear that it wasn't just the apostles who suffered persecution. Ordinary people—like Stephen in Acts 6 and 7— suffered and even lost their lives for righteousness' sake.

6. Read Acts 6:8–15. Why were the Jews antagonistic toward Stephen (verses 8–10)?

7. Stephen answered their charges by preaching a mini-sermon in Acts 7:2–53. How did Stephen show that the Jews had a long history of persecuting the righteous by using the examples of:

Joseph (7:9–10)?

Moses (7:25–29, 35–39)?

Jesus (7:51–52)?

8. Read Acts 7:54–58. What application(s) can you draw from Stephen's example regarding how to handle suffering for righteousness' sake?

9. Read Matthew 5:10–12. What should your attitude be toward those who hate or hurt you? Do Jesus' words apply to any current circumstances in your life? If so, what will you do about it?

10. Pray together for the courage to stand up for what you believe without becoming defensive or compromising your principles.

STUDY FIVE

The School of Suffering

John 11:1–44

Christians down through the centuries have recognized that God often uses pain as an educational tool. God uses suffering in the life of the believer as a means of producing holiness. Paul Powell suggests: "God's goal is not primarily to make us comfortable but to conform us to the image of His Son, Jesus Christ. And in the pursuit of that goal He can and does use all of life's experiences" (*When the Hurt Won't Go Away*, 62). Miles J. Stanford adds that "God does not hurry in His development of our Christian life. He is working from and for eternity!" (*Principles of Spiritual Growth*, 11).

In today's study, Jesus allows a *seeming* tragedy to occur in a family context and uses it as an educational tool. As we explore John 11, pay special attention to the way Jesus uses the circumstances to teach important truths.

1. Does your "track record" indicate that you are a good learner?

2. Read John 11:1–6. What do you think Jesus meant by his affirmation in verse 4?

3. How do you reconcile Jesus' love for Mary, Martha, and Lazarus with his decision to wait for two more days before going to help Lazarus?

4. How do you think Mary and Martha responded when Jesus did not come immediately to help their brother Lazarus? How would you have felt if you were in their shoes?

5. Read John 11:7–16. How do these verses attest to Jesus' deity?

What application can you draw from this regarding God's personal awareness of every hurt you experience?

6. Read John 11:17–37. What do you learn from these verses about Jesus' love and compassion for suffering people?

7. How is the question in verse 37 similar to questions people ask about God today when a tragedy occurs?

8. Read John 11:38–44. What faith-conflict did Martha experience (verses 38–39)?

9. How does Jesus' response to Martha's faith-conflict (verse 40) point back to his affirmation in verse 4?

How does this underscore the importance of trusting God's Word when a tragedy strikes?

10. Meditate a few moments on verses 41–44. How did the final outcome of this ordeal result in much greater glory for Jesus than if he had come earlier to heal Lazarus?

11. What can you learn from this event about what your attitude should be when God delays in answering your prayers?

12. In view of how God can use pain and suffering as an educational tool, what might he be teaching you through a painful circumstance you are facing now?

STUDY SIX

The Chief Culprit

2 Samuel 11:1–17, 26–27; 12:1–13

Pain and suffering began when Adam and Eve sinned against God. In Eden, there was only bliss. They *could* have maintained this pain-free existence; indeed, humanity would *still* be without pain and suffering had sin been avoided. John W. Wenham suggests, "It is probably right to infer that on the biblical view all suffering is ultimately caused by sin of some sort, and that in an unfallen world there would not even be illness, old age and accident such as we experience" (*Enigma of Evil*, 55).

But we *do* live in a fallen world and our lives *are* riddled with pain. Blaine Allen tells us, "Our bodies are contaminated by sin; and as long as we are in them, we will know pain—physically, mentally, and spiritually. That is one of the consequences of being sinners by nature and by choice. Salvation has not changed that. (It will, but not before we see Him face to face.) Thus our God is working with and in a sinful context. The slate will not be wiped clean of sin and its consequences until the appearance of the new heaven and the new earth" (*When God Says No*, 31).

1. Do you think that some people "deserve what they get" when it comes to suffering, while others suffer in life "unfairly"? Why or why not?

In the New Testament, King David is called a man after God's own heart (Acts 13:22). Yet in middle age he fell deeply into sin and *remained* in sin for almost a full year. Things progressively worsened for David until—in desperation—he confessed his sin to God and repented (see Psalm 51).

2. Read 2 Samuel 11:1–5. How do the events described in these verses attest to the importance of "taking the long look" or considering the consequences regarding the decisions one makes in life?

---

3. Read 2 Samuel 11:6–17. How did each of David's actions drive him further and further from God?

How does David's example illustrate what not to do when one sins?

---

4. Read 2 Samuel 11:26–27. After marrying Bathsheba and fathering a son, David probably thought the episode was over and done with. What did he apparently fail to consider (verse 27b)?

---

5. Read 2 Samuel 12:1–10. David "burned with anger" after hearing how the poor man had been abused by the rich man. But Nathan took him off guard when he said, "You are the man!" Why do you think David reacted so strongly in the case of the poor man but was apparently blind to the abhorrence of his *own* actions?

---

6. In what ways had God blessed David (verses 7–8)?

How does this make David's sin that much worse?

7. In verse 9, Nathan asks, "Why did you despise *the word of the Lord* by doing what is evil in his eyes?" Review the Ten Commandments in Exodus 20:1–17. Out of the ten, how many did David break? List them here.

8. Read 2 Samuel 12:11–13. Why does David say "I have sinned against the Lord" when his sin was also against Bathsheba and Uriah?

9. David's confession of sin (verse 13) was made almost a full year after his initial encounter with Bathsheba. Why do you think he took so long in turning back to God?

10. One person's sin can cause many to suffer. Scan through 2 Samuel 11–12:13 again and trace how David's disobedience to God caused pain and suffering for *many* individuals. Pay special attention to verses 11:14–17, 26, 27; and 12:9–12. List your findings below.

11. Though pain and suffering cannot be completely eradicated in this life, how might pain and suffering be *lessened* by obedience to God?

12. What have you learned from David's experience that speaks to your personal situation?

What changes or resolutions do you need to make for the future?

STUDY SEVEN

God's Loving Discipline

Hebrews 12:1–13

In most contexts, the word "discipline" has a negative ring to it. After all, kids don't like being disciplined by parents, and parents don't particularly enjoy disciplining their kids. But imagine what the world would be like if children were never disciplined! Imagine, also, what the spiritual state of Christians would be if God never disciplined them when they went astray.

When God disciplines his children, he doesn't act out of anger or revenge but out of immeasurable love and concern. As Warren W. Wiersbe notes, "our heavenly Father loves us too much to permit us to be rebels, so he chastens us that we might conform to his will . . . God's purpose is not to persecute us, but to perfect us. Chastening is not the work of an angry judge as he punishes a criminal. It is the work of a loving Father as he perfects a child" (*Strategy of Satan*, 45).

1. When you were growing up as a child, how did you usually respond to parental discipline?

2. Read Hebrews 12:1. The "great cloud of witnesses" in this verse refers back to the list of faith heroes in Hebrews 11. Each of them faced tough circumstances, yet all were victorious overcomers because of their faith. What two exhortations are given in view of our being "surrounded" by this "great cloud of witnesses"?

3. How can obeying these instructions minimize the need for God's disciplinary hand in our lives?

4. Read Hebrews 12:2–3. On a practical level, what do you think it means to "fix our eyes" on Jesus?

What dangers are there in aiming our sights too low (like "fixing our eyes" on a Christian leader instead of on Jesus)?

5. According to verse 3, what results can we expect if we fix our eyes on Jesus, even when we are facing tough circumstances?

6. Read Hebrews 12:4–9. Why shouldn't we lose heart when the Lord disciplines us?

7. How is God's discipline in the life of a believer a manifestation of "tough love"?

Martyn Lloyd-Jones suggests: "God's great concern for us primarily is not our happiness but our holiness. In His great love to us He is determined to bring us to that, and He employs many differing means to that end" (*Spiritual Depression*, 235).

8. Read Hebrews 12:10–11. What does God's discipline produce in the life of the believer?

9. Spend a few moments reflecting on your life as a Christian. How have you grown in righteousness as a result of God's loving discipline?

10. Hebrews 12:1–13 is couched in terms of *running a race.*
How does God's discipline provide spiritual "training" for
successfully running this race (verse 11)?

11. Read Hebrews 12:12–13. On a practical level, how could
you go about putting these commands about overcoming sin
into practice?

12. Is it possible that some of the painful circumstances you are
now facing may be explained in terms of God's loving
discipline? Why or why not?

What changes does Hebrews 12:1–13 motivate you to make in
your life at this time?

STUDY EIGHT

The Powers of Darkness

Job 1; 2:1–10; 42:10–17

"Why did this happen to me?"

Ever since the beginning of the human race, people have cried out to God for the answer to this question. The sudden death of a loved one, terminal illness, a car accident, a baby born with a deformity, a devastating tornado—these are just a few of the calamities shared by humankind.

There is perhaps no more potent example of undeserved pain and suffering than Job, a truly upright and godly man. One minute everything was fine in Job's life; the next he had lost nearly everything—his family, his wealth, and his health.

Job had no idea that his body was serving as a spiritual battleground between God and Satan. He was blind to the fact that his suffering was caused by an insidious assault by the powers of darkness, an assault purposefully allowed by a wise and loving God.

1. Have you or someone close to you ever responded to a personal tragedy by asking, "Why did this happen to me?"

2. Read Job 1:1–5. How does the description of Job in this passage show that he was a godly man who had his priorities in proper order?

3. Read Job 1:6–12. What is God's reason for allowing Satan to inflict Job with pain and suffering?

4. Read Job 1:13–19. What do these verses indicate about Satan's ability to motivate other people to harm us? About Satan's ability to use the forces of nature to harm us?

What keeps Satan's power in check? (Review verse 12.)

Warren W. Wiersbe writes, "God was always in control. Satan could not attack Job's possessions until God gave him permission. Satan could not attack Job's person until God allowed it. . . . The one thing God will not control is how we respond to this suffering, and it is here that Satan can gain his purpose" (*Strategy of Satan*, 44).

5. Read Job 1:20–22. How did Job respond to his losses? Is his response consistent with your answer to question 2?

6. Read Job 2:1–10. We saw in Job 1 that Satan can cause suffering by motivating other people to inflict harm and by controlling the forces of nature. What other power does Satan display in Job 2:4–8?

Warren W. Wiersbe notes, "It seemed that all of the calamities in [Job's] life had perfectly natural explanations: the Sabeans took the oxen and donkeys; fire from heaven (perhaps lightning) burned the sheep; the Chaldeans took the camels; and a great wind (a tornado?) wrecked his oldest son's house and killed all of Job's children. But Satan was behind all of them! When God gives him permission, Satan can use people and the forces of nature to accomplish his purposes" (*Strategy of Satan*, 47).

7. What mistake did Job's wife make? What can we learn from her mistake?

8. What can we conclude from Job 1 and 2 about God's character? God's abilities? God's methods?

9. What can we conclude from these chapters about Satan's character? Satan's abilities? Satan's methods?

Chapters 3–31 contain a series of speeches by Job's three friends—Eliphaz, Bildad, and Zophar—and Job's responses. Chapters 32–37 contain four speeches by Elihu, a fourth opinionated counselor. Chapters 38–42 contain two speeches by God and Job's replies. We come to the climax of the story in Job 42:10–17 when God restores Job's prosperity and family.

10. Read Job 42:10–17. Do you think God was obligated to do the things recorded in these verses for Job? In your opinion, would God have been unjust if he hadn't? Why or why not?

11. How should knowing what went on between God and Satan in Job's case affect your response to painful circumstances?

STUDY NINE

Prerequisites for Survival

1 Peter 1:3–25

Moments before her death, martyr Elizabeth Folkes embraced the stake and said, "Farewell, all the world! Farewell, faith; farewell, hope; and welcome love!" Her words conveyed her utter confidence that she would soon be in God's presence where pain and suffering have no place. Faith and hope would no longer be necessary.

During her years on earth, however, the triad of faith, hope, and love were indispensable to her day-to-day spiritual survival. And so it is with each of us. Faith, hope, and love may be considered *prerequisites* for surviving in a world of pain and suffering.

1. The triad of *faith*, *hope*, and *love* occurs often in Scripture. Consider for a few moments what your life might be like if any *one* of these three were missing. How would you survive?

2. Read 1 Peter 1:3–9. What role does *faith* play in seeing us through times of suffering?

What role does *suffering* play in building up our faith muscles?

3. What role does *hope* play in seeing us through times of suffering (verses 3–9)? What is the difference between hope and faith?

4. What role does *love* play in seeing us through times of suffering (verses 8–9)?

5. Read 1 Peter 1:10–12. Faith, hope, and love center on our salvation in Jesus Christ. How is this triad seen in an anticipatory way by the Old Testament prophets who wrote about Christ and his coming redemption of humankind?

6. Read 1 Peter 1:13-16. "Grace" means "unmerited favor."
What do you think it means to "set your hope fully on the grace
to be given you when Jesus Christ is revealed" (verse 13)?

How does this hope relate to obedience to God and personal
holiness (verses 14-16)?

7. Read 1 Peter 1:17-21. What is Peter's admonition in verse
17? How do the truths in verses 18-21 motivate us to be
obedient to this charge?

8. What important truths do verses 17-21 teach you about God?
About Jesus Christ? About faith and hope?

9. Read 1 Peter 1:22-25. How is the Word of God described?

What role does the Word of God play in sustaining faith, hope, and love in the life of a believer?

Charles H. Spurgeon said: "Suffering is meant not only to burn out the dross, but to burn in the promises."

10. As opposed to feeding on the Word of God which endures forever (verse 25), how can investing ourselves in temporal things *dampen* genuine faith, hope, and love in our lives?

11. What have you learned in this study that might help you cope with your present circumstances better?

12. Peter offered praise to God because of the great truths recorded in our passage (verse 3). Based on what you have learned, construct a short prayer of praise to God for his provision of faith, hope, and love in your life.

STUDY TEN

Saved In—Not From

Daniel 3; 6

Believers often experience that God does not save his children *from* tough circumstances, but instead saves them *in* or *through* them. Paul Powell writes: "Though God does not exempt us from suffering and He does not explain to us why our suffering comes, He does enter into our experiences with us and helps us through them. God doesn't save us *from* trouble; he saves us *in* trouble" (*When the Hurt Won't Go Away*, 34).

1. Recall a recent crisis experience in your life. What was your attitude toward God during this time?

2. Read Daniel 3:1–27. Suffering in life is sometimes due to sins we personally commit, but this is not always the case. How does Daniel 3 illustrate that some of our suffering can be due to the sinful activities of other people?

3. What attitude did Shadrach, Meshach, and Abednego display when threatened with being thrown into the blazing furnace (verses 16–18)? What does this say about their priorities?

4. How did King Nebuchadnezzar respond when the three young men refused to give in to his threat (verses 19–23)?

From the human perspective (i.e., *walking by sight*), was there any hope for Shadrach, Meshach, and Abednego?

5. The three young men are called "servants of the Most High God." From what you have read so far, what traits do you see in these three that reflect their commitment to serving God? How do you think this relates to God's willingness to deliver them?

Instead of seeing three men in the furnace, Nebuchadnezzar saw four, and he said the fourth was "like a son of the gods" (verse 25). J. Dwight Pentecost tells us: "This One was probably the preincarnate Christ. Though Nebuchadnezzar did not know of the Son of God, he did recognize that the Person appearing with the three looked supernatural" ("Daniel," *Bible Knowledge Commentary*, 1340).

6. Read Daniel 3:28–30. How does the king answer for himself the question he asked the three men in verse 15, "what god will be able to rescue you from my hand?"

7. In what way does this chapter illustrate the way God often deals with his children in times of trial?

8. Read Daniel 6:1–9. How do these verses illustrate that righteous living does not necessarily insulate one from suffering?

9. Read Daniel 6:10–15. What do you learn about Daniel's priorities in life from verses 10 and 11?

10. Read Daniel 6:16–18. Do you think it likely that Daniel openly shared his faith in God with the king (verse 16)? Why or why not?

11. Read Daniel 6:19–28. What significance do you see in the way the king addressed Daniel early the next morning (verses 19–20)?

12. What do these verses reveal regarding *why* God delivered Daniel?

13. Following this experience, why did the king decree that all the people in his kingdom must fear and reverence the God of Daniel (verses 26–27)?

In both of Daniel's trials, God intervened in a visible way that all could see. It is important for us to recognize, however, that God often helps believers through trials *without physically manifesting His presence.*

14. What do you learn from today's study about what your attitude should be in the midst of a crisis? Of what can you be confident, no matter what circumstances you face in life?

STUDY ELEVEN

When God Says No

2 Corinthians 12:1–10

After God had forbidden Moses to cross the Jordan into the promised land, Moses pleaded with God to change his mind. But God responded, "That is enough. Do not speak to me anymore about this matter. . . . you are not going to cross this Jordan" (Deut. 3:26–27). Moses, one of the greatest spiritual giants in history, was handed a big *NO* from God.

Most Christians receive more *no*'s from God than they care to admit. But God always has his children's highest good in mind when he says *no*. Moreover, he always gives them the grace to accept his *no*'s. Blaine Allen comments: "Never will the Lord say no to a petition without instantly supplying the grace to accept the answer. . . . He will not stockpile it in us in advance, but He will not allow it to be depleted either. Whatever burden He places on us, He will moment by moment carry for us as well" (*When God Says No*, 35).

1. Have you ever asked God to deliver you from some painful experience and received a *no* answer? How did this make you feel? Frustrated? Distant from God? Unspiritual? Confused?

2. Read 2 Corinthians 12:1–6. This passage describes an experience Paul had. Some Bible scholars believe it was when Paul was stoned in Lystra (Acts 14:19) that he was caught up into heaven. How would a supernatural experience like this provide fertile ground for the seed of pride to grow?

3. What do you see in verse 4 that gives you a preliminary indication of why God might want to keep Paul in check in some way?

4. Read 2 Corinthians 12:7–10. How do we know that Paul's suffering was a physical ailment of some kind (verse 7)?

The word for "thorn" (verse 7) carries the idea of "a sharpened wooden shaft," "a stake," or "a splinter." What does this word imply to you about the severity of pain Paul had to endure?

5. The word "torment" (verse 7) literally means "to strike," "to beat," "to harass," or "to trouble." This is the same word used for the soldiers striking and beating Jesus during his trial. Paul's physical ailment was *beating him down*. Despite this, what was God's response when Paul asked him on three occasions to remove it? What was God's greater purpose in Paul's life (verse 7a)?

---

6. Is there any indication that God's refusal to grant Paul's request was related in any way to sin in his life or because of a lack of faith on his part?

Did Paul think the thorn had been given to him for *punishment* or for *protection*?

---

7. The thorn in the flesh was given to Paul by God, but it was administered by Satan (verse 7). Paul knew that God had Satan "on a leash." Instead of rebuking Satan, therefore, what action did Paul take in an effort to have the thorn removed (verse 8)?

8. Originally, Paul probably felt that his ministry would be all the more effective if this thorn were removed from his life. How did his perspective change (verses 9–10)?

9. What do you think God meant when he said to Paul, "My grace is sufficient for you" (verse 9)?

10. If God works best through the weaknesses of his children (verses 9–10), what might be the implications for what he allows to occur in our lives?

11. The word "delight" in verse 10 literally means "to approve" or "to be well pleased with." It refers to an active delighting in God's ways, regardless of the outward circumstances in life. What have you learned in this study that might help you respond this way to weakness and difficulties?

STUDY TWELVE

Helping Those Who Hurt

Luke 10:25–37

After concluding a church service one Sunday evening, a poor man approached young Hudson Taylor and asked him if he would come to his home and pray for his desperately ill wife. Taylor reluctantly agreed, and when he arrived, he was startled at what he saw: "Four or five poor children stood about, their sunken cheeks and temples all telling unmistakably the story of slow starvation; and lying on a wretched pallet was a poor exhausted mother, with a tiny infant thirty-six hours old, moaning rather than crying at her side, for it too seemed spent and failing."

Taylor initially rationalized that he would give this family some money if he only had more. As it was, he had just enough for his meals the next day. But then, says Taylor, "the poor father turned to me and said, 'You see what a terrible state we are in, sir; if you can help us, for God's sake do.' "

Taylor's compassion won out and compelled him to give this family all the money he had. Yet—despite going home with empty pockets—he later reflected: "With peace within and peace without, I spent a happy, restful night." The next morning, Taylor received a monetary gift from an anonymous donor which provided for his food needs the entire week (*Hudson Taylor*, 24).

1. As a Christian, how much helping do you think is *enough* helping in view of the overwhelming number of suffering people in the world?

2. Read Luke 10:25–37. On a practical level, what do you think is involved in loving God with your *whole* being (verse 27)?

3. Scripture views a person's love for other people as a *reflection* of his or her love for God. 1 John 4:20 tells us: "If anyone says, 'I love God,' yet hates his brother, he is a liar. For anyone who does not love his brother, whom he has seen, cannot love God, whom he has not seen." What does this indicate to you about the relationship the priest and the Levite had with God (verses 31–32)?

What insights does this give you on religious hypocrisy?

4. The priest probably could not determine whether the injured man was dead without touching him, which would have made him *ceremonially defiled* (Lev. 21:1ff.). The priest not only refused to help, he went to the other side of the road. Sometimes people commit atrocities for religious reasons. Can you think of some examples from your own experience where someone withheld compassion for religious reasons?

5. What impact do you think Jesus' words had on the Jewish expert in the law, keeping in mind that the hero of the parable was a Samaritan?

6. Jesus indicates in this story that a "neighbor" is *any person with a need that you are able to meet*. What implications does this have for your attitudes and activities regarding the *elderly* in your church or community? Those who are *sick*? Those who are *poor*?

7. The Samaritan gave the innkeeper two silver coins to take care of the wounded man (verse 35). Two silver coins was enough in those days to keep someone in an inn for up to two months. What application can you draw from this part of Jesus' teaching?

8. We learned from verse 27 that Old Testament law is fulfilled by loving God and loving neighbors. Read Galatians 6:2 and summarize how one fulfills the law of Christ.

9. How has the parable of the Good Samaritan helped you to understand what your attitude should be toward those who are suffering?

STUDY THIRTEEN

Paradise Regained

2 Corinthians 4:16–5:10; Revelation 21:1–5

"The Bible begins with a paradise lost and ends with a paradise regained. . . . Not only is it certain that this life will end, but it is certain that from the perspective of eternity it will be seen to have passed in a flash. The toils which seem so endless will be seen to have been quite transitory and abundantly worth while" (*Enigma of Evil*, 55).

Philip Yancey points out the importance of a balanced perspective about our relatively short stay on earth: "In the Christian scheme of things, this world and the time spent here are not all there is. Earth is a proving ground, a dot in eternity—but a very important dot, for Jesus said our destiny depends on our obedience here" (*Where Is God When It Hurts?*, 176).

1. How does the prospect of entering into glory make you feel? Excited? Scared? Ambivalent?

2. Read 2 Corinthians 4:16–18. How can an eternal perspective help us to endure the sufferings of earthly life?

By contrast, how would fixing our eyes on "what is seen" cause us to have a distorted view of human pain and suffering?

3. Read 2 Corinthians 5:1–5. How does 2 Corinthians 5:1 relate to 4:18? How can "fixing our eyes" on our future heavenly body encourage us in the present?

4. In 2 Corinthians 5:5, what does Paul mean when he refers to the Holy Spirit as a "deposit"? Why do you think God gave us the Spirit as a "guarantee" of what is to come?

5. Taken as a whole, what do you think Paul's main point is in 2 Corinthians 5:1–5?

6. Read 2 Corinthians 5:6–10. Why do the truths in verses 6 and 7 belong together?

7. Meditate a few moments on verses 9 and 10. The judgment that Christians look forward to has nothing to do with salvation or loss of salvation. It has only to do with rewards for good works or loss of rewards. How is this truth important in the context of Christians "at home in the body"?

2 Corinthians 4:16–5:10 clearly delineates our present hope as Christians. This hope sustains us during tough times, especially when our bodies experience sickness and pain. It is comforting to know that our heavenly bodies will be pain-free! The Book of Revelation records for us the culmination of human history. We bring our study on human pain and suffering to a close by taking a brief glimpse at what God has in store for us in the eternal state.

8. Read Revelation 21:1–5. According to verse 3, what will be one of the most exciting aspects of living in the eternal state?

9. As a direct result of God's decree, what will be missing from our existence in the eternal state (verse 4)?

10. Why can we be confident of what our future holds (verse 5)?

11. How does knowing what life will be like in the eternal state motivate you to faithfulness in the present?

12. As a result of these studies, what new understandings do you have about "why bad things sometimes happen to good people"?

Leader's Notes

Study One/Paradise Lost

Purpose: to show that humankind's original living environment was a pain-free paradise created by a loving and benevolent God.

Question 2/Eden was a paradise where all physical needs were met (like food, an ideal living environment, esthetic pleasure), and there was perfect fellowship with the Creator since sin had not yet intruded.

Question 3/People can "work for" and "serve" the Creator in many vocations. One does not have to be a member of the clergy to "serve" God. Note that work was part of God's original plan for a perfect world—not a result of the fall. Regardless of vocation, a person's ultimate happiness is derived from serving the Creator.

Question 4/If God intervened every time someone was about to suffer consequences for wrong choices, then people would not truly be free. For God to create human beings with the capacity and freedom to make moral choices, he must by necessity allow them to suffer the consequences for morally wrong choices.

Question 5/God said, "It is not good for the man to be alone" (verse 18). God's provision for intimacy is a heterosexual, monogamous relationship.

Question 6/Satan tried to get Adam and Eve to doubt God's Word and his motives.

Question 7/Adam and Eve's sin alienated them from God. There is pain in all estranged relationships, but an estranged relationship with God is especially painful. The garden was once a place of joy and fellowship with God, but it became a place of fear and of hiding from God.

Question 8/God already knew that Adam and Eve had sinned. When He asks, "Where are you?," his question demonstrates that God seeks people even when they have rebelliously sinned against him.

Question 10/This is a promise that the offspring of the woman (Jesus) would eventually crush the serpent's head. The promise is ultimately fulfilled in Christ's victory over Satan at the cross. God could have destroyed Adam and Eve instantly for their sin. But he displayed goodness and mercy by making provisions for their survival and promising the eventual defeat of Satan.

Question 11/Adam and Eve were banned from their paradise. The rest of their lives were to be lived in a fallen, sinful world. They lost the privilege of walking in the garden in uninterrupted fellowship with God. But God also showed mercy in not allowing them to live forever in such a world. He also made clothes for them and promised the eventual defeat of Satan.

Study Two/Legacy of the Human Race

Purpose: to show the universality of pain and suffering in the human race.

Question 2/The person who seeks meaning in life apart from God is plagued by a perpetual sense of meaninglessness and futility. His very existence causes him pain because he sees no eternal value to what he does in life. The word for "meaningless" originally meant "breath," and referred to that which was fleeting.

Question 3/Solomon first sought refuge in the pursuit of wisdom, thinking that the more he could learn, the less he would suffer. But his pursuit was as "chasing after the wind," a graphic picture of expending effort with no results gained.

Question 5/Solomon's temporality and mortality caused him to despair, and the idea of leaving the fruit of his life's work for someone else to enjoy magnified his pain. The dilemma he was grappling with was: If this life is all there is, then what gives all my efforts in this short life any real meaning?

Question 6/Solomon is not saying that the pursuit of money and material things is wrong in itself. He is simply saying that to pursue these as a means of obtaining *lasting fulfillment* is futile. The hard reality is that no one is around long enough to enjoy the fruit of his labor.

Question 8/The knowledge of our temporality is a kind of pain because we yearn for permanence and eternality. This pain, however, has a positive aspect in that it causes us to seek a relationship with an eternal God. Augustine said: "Thou, O God, hast put eternity in our hearts, and our hearts are restless until they find their rest in thee."

Question 10/The key issue in this passage is *envy* versus *contentment*. Envy causes emotional pain. Contentment brings emotional comfort.

Question 11/The love of money can cause oppression of the poor, lack of rest and sleep, a lack of contentment in life, the barren poverty of having no eternal riches, and the failure to do genuine good in the world with one's riches.

Study Three/A Reflection on God's Character?

Purpose: to show that the existence of pain and suffering in the world is compatible with the fact that the world was created by (and is governed by) a loving and benevolent God.

Question 2/God loves his children too much to remain passive when they stray. A lack of action on God's part would be an indication that he did not love his children. The prophets tell us that Israel was guilty of sin, idolatry, and apostasy. Exile in Babylon was a means God chose to punish his rebellious children.

Question 3/Prolonged suffering is indicated in the psalmist's statement that their lives "ebbed away" because of hunger and thirst. "Ebbed away" is literally "fainted away," a result of prolonged undernourishment.

Question 5/An ancient Jewish commentary on the Old Testament suggests this passage refers to King Zedekiah and the nobles of Judah in exile in Babylon. These individuals found themselves in exile because of rebellion against God's Word.

Question 6/One manifestation of God's unfailing love is that he takes concrete disciplinary action when his children go astray.

Question 8/Emphasize that God *never* disciplines to "get even" with his children. God's purpose is always to *restore* his children to fellowship with him. God allowed these individuals to suffer because they rebelled against his Word. After they repented and cried out to him, he rescued them.

Study Four/Suffering for Righteousness

Purpose: to show that Christians often suffer for doing what is right and for furthering the cause of the gospel.

Question 2/Peter and John were persecuted for teaching that Jesus was resurrected from the dead. The priests were mainly Sadducees, who did not believe in the doctrine of bodily resurrection or in the idea of a personal Messiah. So they had good reason to oppose Peter and John.

Question 3/This is a difficult question and group members may disagree on the answer. Point out that in the context of Acts 4, Peter and John disobeyed the authorities because they believed the Jews were commanding them to do one thing while God had commanded them to do another. They placed God's command above the command of the Jewish authorities.

Question 4/A view held by many Christian leaders is that believers are to submit to all legitimate authorities, even if those authorities are not believers. After all, every authority depends on God for its existence. To disobey a human authority is ultimately to disobey God who ordained the system of human government (Rom. 13:2). Despite this, it is clear that obedience to a human authority must never be in violation of the higher law of God (Acts 4:18–20). To reconcile these passages, a summary principle might be: Christians are to obey man-made laws as long as those laws do not conflict with the clear teaching of Scripture.

Question 5/The believers prayed to God and asked him for boldness to continue serving him in the face of threats by Jewish authorities. They also asked God to perform miracles that would attest to the truth of their words.

Question 8/Stephen was able to have a forgiving attitude because of his relationship with God. He was "full of the Holy Spirit," and his eyes were on the risen Christ. Only as we depend on God can we forgive those who wrong us or persecute us for righteousness' sake.

Study Five/The School of Suffering

Purpose: to show that God sometimes allows suffering in the life of the believer as a means of teaching an important spiritual truth.

Question 2/Jesus did not say that Lazarus would not die but only that the *final outcome* of this sickness would not be death. This episode was to glorify (or manifest the divine perfections of) Jesus in a mighty way. Though no one knew precisely what he meant when he spoke the words recorded in verse 4, Christ would eventually raise Lazarus from the dead—something only God can do. This would testify to Christ's deity before all those present.

Question 3/Human love would no doubt have rushed to the scene of Lazarus's sickness. But divine love—Jesus' love—acts with divine wisdom. Christ deliberately waited for a purpose. He had something to accomplish that no one else was aware of. Jesus' love and his two-day delay are perfectly compatible in view of his divine purpose.

Question 5/In verse 11 Jesus displays the divine attribute of *omniscience.*

Question 8/Martha's conflict was between *walking by sight* and *walking by faith.* By sight, Martha recognized that Lazarus's body had been in the tomb four days, and the body was decaying and stinking. Moreover, to open the tomb would risk becoming defiled. But Martha overcame any doubts and—by an act of faith—obeyed Jesus.

Question 10/Lazarus's resurrection from the dead demonstrated Christ's glory (or divine power) more fully than if Lazarus had simply been healed. Many people put their faith in Christ as a result of this episode.

Study Six/The Chief Culprit

Purpose: to show that a primary cause of pain and suffering in the world is sin.

Question 3/Though one might be able to hide sin from other people, one can never hide sin from God. In David's attempt to hide sin, he committed other sins which drove him further and further from God. When a believer sins, he should immediately confess it to God so fellowship can be restored (1 John 1:9). This doesn't mean temporal consequences for the sin will vanish (e.g., a believer can still go to jail if he robs someone's house). But it does mean that fellowship with God will be restored. Confession of sin to God is always the first step to take.

Question 5/David was so deeply engulfed in sin by this point that he was groping around "in the darkness" and in "blindness." 1 John 2:11 says, "Whoever hates his brother [like David did Uriah] is in the darkness and walks around in the darkness; he does not know where he is going, because the darkness has blinded him." It may also be that David's sin caused his heart to become calloused or hardened to some degree. Psalm 119:70

makes reference to sinners whose hearts are "callous and unfeeling." Such individuals are blind to their own wickedness. Hebrews 3:13 warns believers to avoid becoming "hardened by sin's deceitfulness."

Question 6/It is one thing to own very little and steal from the rich. It is quite another to have vast wealth and steal from the poor. David belonged to this second group, and this made his sin all the worse.

Question 7/Over the course of this episode, David broke four of the ten commandments: "You shall not murder" (Exod. 20:13); "You shall not commit adultery" (Exod. 20:14); "You shall not steal" (Exod. 20:15); "You shall not covet your neighbor's house. You shall not covet your neighbor's wife . . ." (Exod. 20:17).

Question 8/Regardless of other human beings who are on the receiving end of one's actions, all sin is *ultimately* against God. David knew he was guilty of breaking some of the ten commandments. It is with this in mind that he confessed to God: "Against you, you only, have I sinned and done what is evil in your sight" (Psalm 51:4).

Question 9/A person can become enslaved to sin, and this is what happened to David. Jesus said: "I tell you the truth, everyone who sins is a slave to sin" (John 8:34).

Study Seven/God's Loving Discipline

Purpose: to show that God sometimes uses pain and suffering in the life of the believer as a means of discipline.

Question 3/By voluntarily staying away from sin, the believer demonstrates an awareness of God's Word and a commitment to obey it. For such a believer, the *need* for God's discipline is lessened. But even though following the exhortations in this passage can *lessen* the need for God's discipline, there may still be occasions when such discipline is necessary. God is constantly molding his children into the image of Christ. God may accordingly discipline a believer who is not engaged in *conscious* disobedience, but who still has an area in his life that falls short of God's ideal.

Question 4/In the same way a runner concentrates on the finish line, Christians need to concentrate on Jesus. The phrase literally means "to look away from all else, to fix one's gaze upon." It refers not to a casual glance but to a firmly fixed focus on Jesus.

Question 6/Christians should not lose heart when God disciplines them because such discipline is an irrefutable indication that they belong to God's family and are being treated as "sons."

Question 7/God loves his children too much not to intervene when they stray. It grieves God to see his children suffer, especially when they suffer because of his discipline. But God seeks their highest good and will take whatever measures necessary to achieve that good.

Question 10/Just as an athlete trains to stay in good physical shape in order to run a race with optimum efficiency, so the believer runs the Christian race better because of being spiritually trained by God's discipline. But the Christian must make the choice to *allow* himself to be trained by God's discipline.

Question 11/The exhortation implies that the readers are acting as though they were spiritually paralyzed. They are told to shake off whatever weighs them down so they can straighten themselves up again to the full strength of faith. Believers can put these commands into practice by obedience to God's Word, upright conduct, and keeping their eyes focused on Jesus Christ.

Study Eight/The Powers of Darkness

Purpose: to show that Satan has the power and the motive to cause pain and suffering among God's children. A secondary purpose is to show that God limits Satan's activities according to his sovereign will.

Question 3/Satan knew he couldn't deny God's assessment of Job's righteous character. So he made accusations about *why* Job was so pious. He suggested Job was pious because of what he got from God. If these benefits were removed, said Satan, Job would no longer be pious. God allowed Satan to inflict Job with suffering in order to repudiate these false accusations.

Question 4/Satan *can* motivate people to hurt us and *can* use the forces of nature against us—*when God allows him to*. This passage does not imply, however, that every time someone does something bad to another person, it was motivated by Satan. Nor does it imply that every time there is lightning or a tornado, Satan is at work.

Question 5/To tear one's robe symbolized inner turmoil, grief, and shock (cf. Gen. 37:29, 34; 44:13). To shave one's head symbolized the stripping or loss of one's personal glory (cf. Isa. 15:2; Jer. 48:37). These were both considered acts of mourning. Job also "fell to the ground," not in despair but to worship God. His affirmation in verse 21 recognizes God's sovereignty over his life, and he offers praise to God. This response proved Satan's accusation (that Job would curse God and die) utterly wrong.

Question 6/In Job 2:4–8 Satan displays the power to inflict bodily sickness on Job. Again, stress to group members that this is not meant to imply that every time someone gets sick, it is Satan who caused it.

Question 7/Job's wife urged him to "curse God and die." Little did she know that her advice was exactly what Satan had twice predicted Job would do (1:11; 2:5). Job responded by calling her a "foolish woman." "Foolish" literally means "spiritually ignorant," or "undiscerning." Christians must learn to respond to adversity by resting in God's sovereignty. This is especially true when we can't comprehend why adversity has stricken us.

Question 10/God's outpouring of blessing on Job's life after the trial was a token of his *grace*, and not an obligation of his justice.

Study Nine/Prerequisites for Survival

Purpose: to show that one of God's primary provisions for Christians surviving in a world of pain and suffering is the triad of *faith, hope,* and *love.* These three strands form a powerful rope that acts as a lifeline to God.

Question 3/Faith and hope are closely related but different. *Faith* rests wholly upon the facts of Scripture. It is a confident belief that what God has told us is completely true. *Hope* refers to the eager looking forward to our eternal, glorious future with an expectant attitude and a confidence of its fulfillment.

Question 4/The love for Christ which Peter speaks of indicates that the focus of a believer's faith is not on abstract knowledge or data, but on the *living person of Jesus Christ*. It is this personal relationship that has sustaining power for the Christian in difficult circumstances. Our love for God sustains us in times of suffering. So too, does brotherly love among Christians.

Question 5/*Faith* is seen in the prophets' belief in the future Messiah who would suffer and then enter glory. *Hope* is seen in their interest and excitement about God's broad plan of salvation centering on the coming Messiah. *Love* is seen in their devotion and service to God and their obedience to "the spirit of Christ in them."

Question 6/Scholars are not in full agreement here. Many believe this verse refers to the grace or "unmerited favor" of final deliverance from sin and the blessedness of finally being in Christ's presence in glory.

Question 7/The shedding of Christ's blood was a perfect and complete sacrifice for the sins of humankind. He was a perfect Lamb, without blemish or spot. Before Adam and Eve fell, indeed before people were even created, it was ordained that Christ would shed his blood for humanity's sins. This fact, however, was revealed only "in these last times for your sake" (1 Peter 1:20). All this should prompt us to unrestrained faithfulness, living our lives as strangers here in reverent fear.

Question 9/God's Word is eternal and stands forever; therefore, believers have a solid rock on which to anchor their faith.

Study Ten/Saved In—Not From

Purpose: to show the biblical pattern of God saving his children *in* (or *through*) painful circumstances, not *from* painful circumstances.

Question 2/Too often, well-meaning Christians assume that when they see a believer suffering, it is an indication of sin and God's discipline. This passage, however, indicates that suffering is often rooted in the sinful activities of *other* people. Christians must be cautious not to cast judgment on a suffering believer, pronouncing a "guilty verdict" without knowing the facts.

Question 3/Daniel and his friends trusted in God's *sovereignty*. Because of this, they told the king they didn't need to defend themselves in this matter. They also acknowledged God's *omnipotence*, telling the king that God had power to save them from the fiery furnace. Their mindset was one of total *faithfulness and obedience to God*, regardless of the outcome.

Question 5/As servants of God, Daniel and his friends recognized that God's authority was greater than Nebuchadnezzar's authority. They were *employed* by Nebuchadnezzar; they *served* Yahweh. A primary characteristic of a good servant is unflinching obedience, regardless of what is requested. Daniel and his friends were model servants in this regard. For Daniel and his friends to worship the false gods and bow down before the image of gold would have been the same as *serving* false gods. As servants of the true God, they refused to do this.

Question 7/If God had wanted to, he could have intervened earlier and prevented the three youths from being thrown into the furnace. But he chose not to do this.

Question 8/The life of Christ in the New Testament is the greatest illustration in Scripture of how righteous living does not insulate one from suffering.

Question 9/When Daniel became aware of the new decree, he went straight home and did the very thing forbidden by the decree. His priorities remained unchanged. Daniel was now about 80 years of age. How could he now deny the God who had been so faithful to him all his life? The content of Daniel's prayer also reveals his priorities. Instead of praying fearfully, Daniel begins by offering *thanksgiving* to God. Then he calmly asks God for guidance and help in dealing with the new dilemma.

Question 10/This is a speculative question. It seems likely, however, that Daniel shared his faith in God with King Darius because Daniel was very open about being a servant of God.

Question 11/Darius calls Daniel a servant of the *living* God. In Scripture, references to the "living God" occur in contexts where God is seen as one who intervenes in the lives of his people. God is not a distant deity. He is very much present and active in the affairs of his children.

Study Eleven/When God Says No

Purpose: to examine the proper Christian response when God says *no* to a prayer request for deliverance from undesirable circumstances.

Question 2/Paul actually saw "the third heaven," the dwelling place of Christ and the saints. This glorious experience would likely have tempted him to boast about it pridefully, especially when his apostleship was challenged by some in Corinth.

Question 4/Paul's suffering was called a "thorn *in the flesh*." The word "flesh" is the normal word in the Greek used to denote the physical substance of which the body is composed.

Question 7/Instead of rebuking Satan, Paul addressed himself to "the Lord." His prayer was directed to his risen Master, the Lord Jesus Christ, who on the cross defeated Satan and openly displayed this victory as he ascended into heaven. Contrary to the contemporary emphasis of rebuking demons for suspected activity here and there, our primary focus should be on the Lord Jesus Christ. After all, "the one who is in you is greater than the one who is in the world" (1 John 4:4).

Question 8/Before, Paul probably boasted in strength. Now he boasts in his weakness, for when he is weak, Christ's power is all the more abundantly showered on him. Experiences he formerly would have abhorred, he could now welcome supernaturally because the evidence of Christ's power in the midst of them brought glory to God, not Paul.

Question 9/This verse means that the greater the Christian's acknowledged weakness, the more evident Christ's enabling strength (cf. Eph. 3:16; Phil. 4:13). The tense indicates continuous, linear action. God's grace is *continually sufficient* for whatever comes up in life.

Study Twelve/Helping Those Who Hurt

Purpose: to show that all Christians are called upon to be people-helpers.

Question 3/A Christian's *deeds*, not his *words*, are the true indicator of his relationship with God. Anyone can say "I love God" (like the Priest and Levite). But only those who have taken God's commands to heart will allow that love to be reflected in the way they treat others.

Question 5/This is a speculative question. But in view of the antagonism Jews felt toward Samaritans, it is likely that the Jewish expert in the law found the parable difficult to digest. Jews considered Samaritans half-breeds, both *physically* (Matt. 10:5) and *spiritually* (John 4:20, 22). On top of this, the villains of the parable were the Priest and the Levite.

When Jesus asked him, "Which of these three do you think was a neighbor to the man who fell into the hands of the robbers?" (Luke 10:36), the law expert apparently found it too difficult to say the word *Samaritan*. He could only respond, The one who had mercy on him."

Study Thirteen/Paradise Regained

Purpose: to show that Christians will eventually be "free at last" from the pain and suffering of mortal existence, and that paradise will be regained because of what Christ has accomplished in their behalf.

Question 2/Focusing only on what is seen leads to a distorted understanding of human pain and suffering. Such a perspective is reminiscent of human existence "under the sun" as described by Solomon in Ecclesiastes, resulting in meaninglessness and despair. Only by focusing on the *unseen realities* of the spiritual realm and future glory are we able to keep pain and suffering in proper perspective.

Question 3/Because of our faith in the *unseen reality* of our future glorified bodies (bodies that are *pain*-free, *decay*-free, and *death*-free), we can derive strength to cope with present sicknesses, pain, and death.

Question 4/The word "deposit" was used among the Greeks to refer to a pledge which guaranteed final possession of an item. It was sometimes used of an engagement ring which acted as a guarantee that the marriage would take place. The Holy Spirit is a "deposit" in the sense that his presence in our lives guarantees our eventual total transformation and glorification into the likeness of Christ's glorified body (cf. Phil. 3:21).

Question 5/No matter what we as Christians are facing, we have a *hope* in what lies ahead in eternity. Regardless of the condition of our mortal bodies, we have heavenly bodies awaiting us that will never ail again.

Question 6/As long as the believer is at home in the body and away from the Lord, he must live in this fallen, sinful, temporal world *by faith* and not *by sight*. Walking by sight would only lead to despair and meaninglessness in life. Walking by faith leads to hope in the future life.

Question 7/The fact that Christians will receive or lose rewards for their actions on earth in their mortal lives is a strong motivation for faithfulness and obedience to God while we are "at home in the body."

Question 8/One of the greatest things Christians have to look forward to in the eternal state is that God will dwell with them forever. There will be no more separation because of sin, for sin will be no more.

Question 9/Paul W. Powell comments: "There will be no blind eyes in heaven. No withered arms or legs in heaven. No pain or agony there. Tears will be gone. Death will be gone. Separation will be gone. This will be the ultimate healing. Then and only then, we will be free at last" (*When the Hurt Won't Go Away*, 119).

Bibliography/ Recommended Reading

Allen, Blaine, *When God Says No*. Nashville: Thomas Nelson, 1981.

Anderson, Norman, *The Teaching of Jesus*. Downers Grove, IL: InterVarsity Press, 1982.

Apichella, Michael, *Not What I Expected: When the Christian Life Seems to Fail*. Wheaton, IL: Shaw, 1989.

Calvin, John, *Institutes of the Christian Religion*, edited by John T. McNeill. Philadelphia: Westminster Press, n.d.

Elliot, Elisabeth, *Shadow of the Almighty*. Grand Rapids, MI: Zondervan, 1977.

Geisler, Norman L., *The Roots of Evil*. Grand Rapids, MI: Zondervan, 1978.

Lewis, C. S., *The Problem of Pain*. New York: Macmillan, 1975.

Littleton, Mark. *When God Seems Far Away*. Wheaton, IL: Shaw 1987.

Lloyd-Jones, D. Martyn, *Spiritual Depression: Its Causes and Cure*. Grand Rapids, Eerdmans, 1976.

Pentecost, J. Dwight, "Daniel," in *The Bible Knowledge Commentary*, Old Testament, edited by John F. Walvoord and Roy B. Zuck. Wheaton, IL: Victor Books, 1985.

Pentecost, J. Dwight, *The Parables of Jesus*. Grand Rapids, MI: Zondervan, 1982.

Powell, Paul W., *When the Hurt Won't Go Away*. Wheaton, IL: Victor Books, 1986.

Ross, Allen P., "Genesis," in *The Bible Knowledge Commentary*, Old Testament, edited by John F. Walvoord and Roy B. Zuck. Wheaton, IL: Victor Books, 1985.

Sauer, Erich, *In the Arena of Faith*. Grand Rapids, MI: Eerdmans, 1977.

Stanford, Miles J., *Principles of Spiritual Growth*. Lincoln, NE: Back to the Bible, 1976.

Taylor, J. Hudson, *Hudson Taylor*. Minneapolis, MN: Bethany House, n.d.

Wenham, John W., *The Enigma of Evil*. Grand Rapids, MI: Zondervan, 1985.

Wiersbe, Warren W., *The Strategy of Satan*. Wheaton, IL: Tyndale House, 1980.

Yancey, Philip, *Disappointment with God*. Grand Rapids, MI: Zondervan, 1989.

_____, *Where is God When It Hurts?* Grand Rapids, MI: Zondervan, 1977.

Zuck, Roy B., *Job*, Everyman's Bible Commentary. Chicago: Moody Press, 1978.

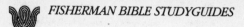 FISHERMAN BIBLE STUDYGUIDES

Check your local bookstore or write **Harold Shaw Publishers, Box 567, Wheaton, Illinois**